# STEP FORWARD WITH
# PROBLEM SOLVING

SHANNON WELBOURN

Crabtree Publishing Company

www.crabtreebooks.com

# STEP FORWARD!

**Author**
Shannon Welbourn

**Series research and development**
Reagan Miller

**Editorial director**
Kathy Middleton

**Editors**
Reagan Miller, Janine Deschenes

**Series Consultant**
Larry Miller: BA (Sociology), BPE, MSc.Ed
Retired teacher, guidance counselor, and certified coach

**Print and production coordinator**
Katherine Berti

**Design and photo research**
Katherine Berti

**Photographs**
Getty Images: Gary Gershoff, p 17
Shutterstock: ©Benoit Daoust, p 15 (left); © Chris102, p 18
Other images by Shutterstock

**Library and Archives Canada Cataloguing in Publication**

Welbourn, Shannon, author
    Step forward with problem solving / Shannon Welbourn.

(Step forward!)
Includes index.
Issued in print and electronic formats.
ISBN 978-0-7787-2768-2 (hardback).--ISBN 978-0-7787-2808-5
(paperback).--ISBN 978-1-4271-1826-4 (html)

    1. Problem solving--Juvenile literature.  I. Title.

BF449.W35 2016          j153.4'3          C2016-903351-1
                                          C2016-903352-X

**Library of Congress Cataloging-in-Publication Data**

CIP Available at the Library of Congress

## Crabtree Publishing Company

www.crabtreebooks.com          1-800-387-7650

Printed in Canada/102016/IH20160811

**Published in Canada**
**Crabtree Publishing**
616 Welland Ave.
St. Catharines, Ontario
L2M 5V6

**Published in the United States**
**Crabtree Publishing**
PMB 59051
350 Fifth Avenue, 59th Floor
New York, New York 10118

**Published in the United Kingdom**
**Crabtree Publishing**
Maritime House
Basin Road North, Hove
BN41 1WR

**Published in Australia**
**Crabtree Publishing**
3 Charles Street
Coburg North
VIC 3058

# CONTENTS

# WHAT IS PROBLEM SOLVING?

**There are more than 7 billion people in the world. What is one thing we all have in common? We all face problems!**

Whether they are old, young, rich, or poor, everyone faces problems. Problems are obstacles or challenges that get in the way of our **goals** and activities. They may be small, such as a computer game not working, or much bigger, such as getting lost in a new place. When you encounter a problem, you need to find a way around it. That means you need to find a **solution**.

*Problem solving is a skill that we gain and get better at over time. We use it every day.*

You may also be faced with **conflicts**. A conflict is what happens when two or more people have different points of view on what to do or how to do something. You and some friends might be working on a puzzle when you disagree on where to fit a piece. You think it belongs in the middle of the puzzle, but your friend thinks it should fit at the top. Resolving conflicts tests your problem-solving skills. Finding a solution requires **patience**. It takes skill to solve the problem so that everyone feels satisfied that the solution is fair.

# WHY IS PROBLEM SOLVING IMPORTANT?

**Being a good problem solver is an important skill to have. It will help you in many parts of your life.**

Everyone faces problems at times in their lives. Sometimes problems cause **stress**. Arguing with a friend or having a hard time with schoolwork can make people feel worried and upset. Sometimes, problems can cause people to feel unwell and have trouble sleeping. Having good problem-solving skills makes it easier to deal with problems. Being able to solve problems helps us avoid stress.

*It can be challenging to resolve a conflict. Finding a solution can take time!*

*Problem solving helps us feel capable and **resourceful**.*

It is important to remember that most problems have solutions. Some problems can be solved quickly, while others are more difficult and can take time. Either way, it is important to know that things will improve over time.

*Problem solving can help us resolve problems quickly and avoid getting angry.*

# STEPS TO PROBLEM SOLVING

**It can be difficult to tackle a problem. Try these steps to break the problem into small parts and find a solution.**

**1**

Start by figuring out what the problem actually is, so you have a clear understanding of what you need to solve. To help define the problem, think about these questions:

• What do I want?
• What is stopping me from getting what I want?
• How am I feeling? Why do I feel this way?

*You and your brother argue over whose turn it is to play on the computer. You think about the problem. You want to play your favorite computer game, and you feel upset.*

**2**

Often there are several ways to solve the same problem. Think of as many ways as you can to solve the problem. **Brainstorm** ideas by yourself or with others.

*You come up with some solutions with your brother, such as splitting up the computer time equally, letting your brother play because he is older, and playing together.*

Choose a solution that seems like it will work the best. Think about the effects of that solution. Try using these questions to help you:

- How will my solution affect others? Is it fair to them? How will it make them feel?
- Is my solution safe?
- Will my solution create any new problems?

*You decide to try playing together. You and your brother agree that this is safe and fair to both of you.*

Try your solution. After you've tried it, go back and check to see if your solution solved the problem. If it did not help, try a different solution from your list.

*After playing one round of the game, you think back to the original problem. Both you and your brother are able to play on the computer. You do not feel upset anymore. Your solution worked!*

# PROBLEM SOLVING AT HOME

Community

School

Home

**Each family is unique and has different needs. There are many ways you can help to solve problems at home.**

At home, you work together with your family to solve problems. Maybe many members of your family share a bathroom. This may cause problems when everyone is getting ready for school and work in the morning. You think of some ways that you could help to solve this problem. You arrange a family meeting so everyone can share their ideas to solve the problem. Your father suggests creating a morning schedule. Your sister offers to shower the night before. You suggest waking up earlier to have more time.

It is important for everyone to be **respectful** and listen to others' ideas. The needs of each member of the family need to be met. Your family decides to follow a morning bathroom schedule. You also decide to wake up 15 minutes earlier each day. This makes sure everyone can use the bathroom every morning.

*Being a good listener is important for solving problems. Everyone should have a chance to talk.*

# PROBLEM SOLVING AT SCHOOL

Community

School

Home

**You spend a lot of time at school. Learning problem-solving skills can help you make school the best place it can be.**

You are playing with a friend during recess when you notice that a girl is being picked on by her classmates. You know that bullying is a very serious problem. You also know that serious problems such as bullying are too big to solve on your own.

*You should talk to teachers, parents, or other trusted adults about problems that affect the safety or health of you and others.*

You decide to ask your teacher for help to solve the problem. It is important to ask someone you trust for help solving problems. Your teacher speaks with the girl, her classmates, and her parents. You and your friend also decide to help solve the problem by standing up against the bullies. Solving this problem takes many solutions put together!

## STEP FURTHER

Who are some people in your life that you trust to ask for help solving problems?

# PROBLEM SOLVING IN YOUR COMMUNITY

Community

School    Home

**A community is a group of people who live, work, and play in a place. Your home, school, and neighborhood are part of your community.**

All communities have problems that need solutions. People in communities work together to solve problems. Kids like you can get involved in solving problems and making your community a better place to live. Some people may not have enough warm clothing to wear during winter months. You could help collect coats and mittens to **donate**. There may be a lot of litter in your community. You could help solve this problem by taking part in a community clean-up project.

Some communities have outdoor libraries for people to borrow books. You could help create one in your community to help families who cannot afford to buy books. If your community already has one, you could help organize a book drive to donate books to the library.

*You are never too young to help solve problems in your community. When people help to solve problems, communities are better places to live.*

# JAYLEN ARNOLD

**Name:** Jaylen Arnold

**From:** Lakeland, Florida

**Accomplishment:** Solved bullying problems at his school and encourages anti-bullying around the world.

**For years Jaylen Arnold was faced with the problem of bullying at his school. He decided to stand up and solve the problem...for kids everywhere.**

Jaylen has different abilities than most kids. He has Tourette Syndrome, which means that his body sometimes moves when he doesn't want it to. He also has **Asperger Syndrome** and **Obsessive Compulsive Disorder**. These affect the way he interacts with people. Because he is different, Jaylen was bullied at school. When he was 8 years old, he decided to speak up against bullying. He set a goal that he would spread his anti-bullying message on the Internet and television. Putting a stop to bullying is a huge challenge, but Jaylen didn't give up. He asked his family, friends, and other trusted adults for help to spread his message.

With help, Jaylen created a website and achieved his goal by launching Jaylen's Challenge, an organization that promotes anti-bullying messages through education and community service. Today, Jaylen speaks to youth around the world on the Internet and on television. He believes that if everyone works together, we can solve the problem of bullying!

*In 2014, Jaylen was honored with the World of Children award for speaking out against bullying everywhere.*

"Kids...[at my school] love me for who I am. I want ALL kids to experience the same feeling. I am going to do my best to make that happen!"

—Jaylen Arnold

# OVERCOMING CHALLENGES

**Sometimes, we might want to ignore a difficult problem rather than trying to find a solution.**

Most problems do not just go away on their own. Some problems can get bigger if you ignore them. It is important to believe that you can find a solution. Remember these helpful problem-solving tips to get you started:

**When you face a problem...**

- Think positively. Every problem can be solved with time. Believe in yourself and remember that practicing problem-solving skills is more important than getting it perfect every time.

- Ask yourself if you have ever faced a similar problem in the past. If so, how did you solve it? Could you use a similar solution for your current problem?

- Break down your problem into smaller parts. What are some small steps you can take to move toward a solution?

It is important to try to solve problems on your own. But some problems may be too big to tackle by yourself. Sometimes finding a solution takes teamwork. Sharing a problem with family or friends can help you feel less stress. They may see your problem from a different point of view or offer suggestions for new solutions.

STEP
FURTHER

Can you think of a time you used teamwork to solve a problem?

**Once you have practiced your problem-solving skills, you can help others to be good problem solvers too.**

When you or someone you know encounters a problem, encourage others to brainstorm with you. Make sure they feel welcome to share their solutions by listening to them respectfully. Even if you disagree with a solution, every idea is important and we all bring a different point of view to the problem. Often one idea can grow into many ideas. Finding solutions to problems helps us to feel hopeful that any problem we face can be solved!

*It's important to learn to solve problems by yourself and with other people. Practice your teamwork while you solve problems!*

# PROBLEM SOLVING IN ACTION

**Everyone faces problems from time to time. Building problem-solving skills can help you feel more capable and free of stress.**

Read the example below. Which boy is following the problem-solving steps? You can review the steps on pages 8–9.

Nathan and Mika agree to work as partners on a class project. They are almost done, but the boys disagree on the best way to complete the project. Nathan feels upset. He knows he could finish the project if Mika did not disagree with him. Mika suggests they put their ideas together and come up with a way of solving the problem they can both agree on. Instead, Nathan decides to use his own idea without telling Mika. He finishes their project and hands it in to the teacher.

What was the boys' goal?

What was the problem?

Will both boys be happy with the solution?

Which boy followed the problem-solving steps? Explain your thinking.

# LEARNING MORE

## BOOKS

Burstein, John. *Why are You Picking on Me? Dealing with Bullies*. Crabtree Publishing, 2010.

Burstein, John. *Can We Get Along? Dealing with Differences.* Crabtree Publishing, 2010.

Cohen, Marina. *Live It: Cooperation.* Crabtree Publishing, 2010.

## WEBSITES

**http://pbskids.org/games/problem-solving**
Try out your problem-solving skills with these fun, interactive games at the PBS kids website.

**www.pacerkidsagainstbullying.org/kab**
Connect with other kids and learn about what you can do to help solve the problem of bullying in schools across North America.

**www.jaylenschallenge.org**
Learn more about Jaylen Arnold, his story, and his problem-solving activism at his website.

# WORDS TO KNOW

**Asperger Syndrome** [AS-per-ger] noun  A type of autism—a disorder that affects how the brain works

**brainstorm** [BREYN stawrm] verb  The act of quickly coming up with and recording ideas without judging them, often done in a group

**conflicts** [KON-flikts] noun  A clash or incompatible difference of ideas, interests, or goals

**donate** [DOH-neyt] verb  To make a free gift or contribution toward a cause

**goals** [gohls] noun  The aim toward which effort is directed

**Obsessive Compulsive Disorder** [*uh* b-SES-iv k*uh* m-PUHL-siv] noun  An anxiety disorder that causes people to have repeated thoughts and actions

**patience** [PEY-sh*uh* ns] noun  The ability to endure boredom or frustration

**resourceful** [ri-SAWRS-f*uh* l] adjective  Describing someone who is able to use different methods to solve problems or achieve goals

**respectful** [ri-SPEKT-f*uh* l] adjective  Describing someone who is polite and gives appropriate attention to others

**solution** [s*uh*-LOO-sh*uh* n] noun  The act or process of solving a problem

**stress** [stres] noun  The body's response to fear, pain, worry, and other situations, causing negative effects to health

# INDEX

# ABOUT THE AUTHO

Shannon Welbourn is a freelance author of educational K-12 books. She holds an hono BA in Child & Youth Studies, and is a certifie teacher. Shannon works full-time as a Libra and Media Specialist. In this position, she works closely with teachers and teacher candidates, helping to inspire and devel a passion for learning. Shannon lives c to Niagara Falls and enjoys vacationi in the Muskokas with her family.